Growth Hungry Brand Managers
In Bathroom Sanitaryware Industry

PUT YOUR *Instagram* ON FORMULA ONE FAST TRACK

Discover the core reasons for your slow growth and what can put your growth on fast track

Growth Hungry Brand Managers
In Bathroom Sanitaryware Industry

PUT YOUR Instagram ON FORMULA ONE FAST TRACK

Discover the core reasons for your slow growth and what can put your growth on fast track

NITIN GUPTA

Worldwide Published by
Pendown Press

PENDOWN PRESS
An ISO 9001 & ISO 14001 Certified Co.,
Regd. Office: 2525/193, 1st Floor, Onkar Nagar-A,
Tri Nagar, Delhi-110035
Ph.: 09350849407, 09312235086
E-mail: info@pendownpress.com
Branch Office: 1A/2A, 20, Hari Sadan, Ansari Road,
Daryaganj, New Delhi-110002
Ph.: 011-45794768
Website: PendownPress.com

First Edition: 2023
ISBN: 978-93-5554-479-7

Layout and Cover Designed by Pendown Graphics Team

This book is dedicated to my mentor Akshar Yadav. It wouldn't have come into existence without his continuous motivation and guidance.

Contents

-1-

Social Media: The Way to Success

"Social media is not just media. The key is to listen, engage, and build relationships."

~David Alston

So, friends, let's start this conversation by looking at the current business environment.

It has always been said, "Only that which is visible sells well." This means that connecting with your customers is essential to business success so that they know you and see you.

Today the world is digital, and so is the marketplace. In the current scenario, being visible means connecting with your customers via social media platforms.

Having an active and effective social media presence has become vital to the extent that, like project management companies, today, we have social media management companies, literally in truckloads.

Youngsters with fancy degrees making big promises and creating complex social media strategies are in abundance. In some cases, the main line popular P.R. or advertising agency may be handling the social media account also.

However, I want you to stop and think for a moment,

Is it working for you?

Most times, these agencies are coming up with new customer engagement ideas, and they are doing everything in their power but are unable to engage people in the same proportions as their name in the market and the whopping amount of marketing budget they eat up.

So, what happens in such a scenario? You can't keep going on hit & trial mode; of course, you can't change an agency every year. Imagine your plight: you have hired the best agency, yet they are not performing. You are following the creative director, so it is not your fault. However, at the end of it all, it is you who are answerable to the management.

However, what happens is that at the end of it all, there are no or less tangible results from social media. Recession is looming large over businesses, and budgets need to be tight. Obviously, social media is the first to take the hit in such situations.

Precious marketing budget is going down the drain; people are not engaging, no matter what content you are posting. A handful of likes, and that too mostly from your own dealer network, company employees are your only consolation, while **actual external followers are only a handful and growing at a snail's pace.**

The poor results are spoiling your track record and tarnishing your credibility, especially when there is a possibility. When there is a market leader who is growing leaps and bounds, and you are not. **You're playing safe & it's going against your growth, my friend.**

And the worst part is that in the process, you stop focusing on social media; your most powerful and promising tool...

But fear not, there is a way out, and to show you that way is the intent behind writing this book, so let's dive in further…

-2-

Right Questions Lead to Right Answers

"Asking questions is the first way to begin change."

~Kubra Sait

If you are getting poor results, and poor answers, then it means the questions you are asking are not the right ones.

How do I increase my brand followers is the wrong question to ask?

Let me repeat.

How do I increase my brand followers is the wrong question to ask?

If you want to put an end to all the struggle and pain of followers growing at a snail's pace and transform your life, then:

You must ask the right questions.

Okay, I know what you are thinking, "Nitin, when we are talking about social media, how is this a wrong question to ask?"

Let me explain: your question is not entirely wrong, but you are just looking at the surface and not digging deep. What you need to do is reframe the question and approach the situation from a different perspective.

Here is a list of the questions to ask from a solution and action-based approach:

1. What is not working for my social media & why is it not working? **(In the context of getting followers in abundance)**
2. What is working & why is it working?
3. How can I add value to my audience?
4. Why should they follow us?
5. Is my content evoking positive emotions?
6. Is it bringing a smile to the face and a glow in the eyes of my audience?
7. What is the market leader doing that is getting them results?

When we ask the right questions, the whole game changes.

The direction becomes different. The thought patterns and ideas become different. The actions become different, and you start getting the results that you want.

-3-

Content Is Not King; Intent is

"Content is useless without the Correct Intent."

-Nitin Gupta, Out-of-the-box Design Thinking Expert

So when we ask the right questions, we are led to the answer that if we want followers... we should have content that people should like.

- **Which means it all boils down to the Content.**
- **Right?**
- **Wrong!**

At this point, again, you must be doubting what I am saying, but like earlier, here, too, we need to go deeper. Let me ask you a question. A question perhaps no one has ever asked you before.

What is your intent behind your content?

Here are the possible answers:

a. Grow followers

b. Get likes

- **c.** Ego massage your product influencers, such as architects and designers
- **d.** Just to create a content pipeline and meet the KRA.
- **e.** Tell them about the features of your product

  (Rarely have I seen content on a Bathroom Fitting brand's page that is about **adding value to the lives of their audience.**)

The **CORE problem** is at the source: **The Intent.**

"Content is useless without the Correct Intent."

A substandard intent will produce substandard content. Substandard content can never produce the desired results.

The biggest mistake any brand or business makes is not creating content with the right intent of adding value to their customer's/follower's life.

Sadly, today, it has all become a number game. So many videos and so many festival posts. Just a number game. Just ticking the box so that the KRA of posting daily is met.

That's it.

But that's it is not good enough.

For your social media to thrive and convert into a customer engaging platform with hundred thousands of followers generating qualified leads and business as a bonus, you must create conscious content with the intent of adding value.

In the following chapters, I will share with you in detail about the kind of content that is being created versus what actually works, all the categories of content and million-dollar tips on creating transformative content that works like magic.

-4-

Who am I & Why Should You Listen to Me?

"Identifying and breaking patterns that do not serve you, is the first step towards success. The rest follows."

-Nitin Gupta, Out-of-the-box Design Thinking Expert

Okay, let me introduce myself; you must be wondering who I am and how I am so sure of what I am talking about.

Well, to put it briefly, I am so sure of the transformative value I am sharing through this book because I have been part of a leading Bathroom Fittings brand's miraculous growth journey on social media by practically implementing their idea of creating 3D Bathroom Inspirations for them. **This helped them grow from 10k followers to 300k followers in just 3 years.**

Hello, my name is Nitin Gupta, and I run a creative agency, The Next Design.

I am an Interior Designer turned entrepreneur with a strong background in 3D technologies, Design and a God's gift for seeing upcoming Technology Trends ahead of time.

I have been running The Next Design, with 3D as its strongest muscle, since 2004, helping global brands solve their unique problems. Whether it is about creating virtual airports, power plants, or showrooms or creating creative content for boosting social media followers, I enjoy solving problems and adding value in the realm of marketing.

I am thankful to my clients for having faith in me and trusting me to solve their biggest challenges, to my family for supporting me in all ups and downs and to the Universe for blessing me with this life purpose of helping others flourish.

I am incredibly grateful to my mentor Akshar Yadav for inspiring me to write this book and share my experience and expertise with business owners, especially Bathroom Fittings brands, to empower them to connect with their audience resulting in exponential success and profits.

This book is specifically for growth-hungry Brand Managers who are struggling to reach the 100k followers mark despite their best efforts and hiring expensive, top agencies for years. It is for all those who aspire to take their brand to this level in the shortest possible time.

With so much corporate pressure to perform and deliver instantaneously, it is sometimes difficult to see things from a different lens. **That's precisely what I am doing via this book.** I am helping you change the lens and view things from a unique perspective. Once you change the lens, clarity emerges. With this shift in perspective, you'll be able to see the mistakes that have been stopping you from reaching 100k followers till now.

So how did I reach this landmark where I am equipped to empower and benefit others with my skill and learning acquired over the years?

A Dream Shattered-A Promise Made

Let me start at the beginning. Since childhood, I had a dream of becoming an architect but unfortunately I was scared of science in school and opted for commerce. My dream was shattered. But in spite of the heartbreak and disappointment, my intent did not waver and as I have already shared earlier, the intent is the king. Then & there, **I committed to myself that even though I couldn't become an architect, I would still go on to do big projects.**

And when our intent is strong, results automatically follow, whether on social media or in life.

I was in 11th grade, and one day on a Sunday afternoon, I went to visit a friend of mine. There I saw him working on his computer, and I saw a real-looking, life-like image of a metal bucket with dazzling sunlight falling on it. That sparkling image is still so vivid in my memory.

I came home mesmerized and asked my brother, who was doing engineering, if I could get the software that had made rendering that image possible.

I was fortunate to have a brother like him (I still am) and a computer at home, and he gave me a photocopied manual of 3D Studio. It used to be DOS based in 1995. **And that was the beginning of my journey in 3D. The journey that has brought me to this book and my mission of helping Bathroom Fittings brands leverage the power of social media.**

After completing school, the normal course for a commerce graduate was to go in for B.COM and/or C.A. Following the trend, I too enrolled in B.COM and tried giving C.A papers. But, it was so not my cup of tea. I could not even copy from the book. I tore up the papers, and in that moment, I knew I was in the wrong lane.

I then tried my hands at Interior Design, and that's something I instantly liked and loved. It was colors and design, and it fitted me as if it was a part of me. With this career path, the Universe had rewarded my intent and put me in alignment with my dream of being an architect and doing big projects.

I completed my interior design program and worked with a leading architect for 2 years and was part of the team that designed and built Pizza Hut and Baristas. However, there came the point when I saw that the learning had stopped. I quit and started The Next Design.

Fast-Faster-Racing to the Top

At Next Design, it gave me great delight as I used to show people how their office, home or commercial building would look in 3D, and soon, I built my website, www.thenextdesign.com.

I learnt about google ads and SEO in 2005 and realized that this was my gateway to success. I started getting projects from all over the world. I got a Bank of America Corporate office animation project for 20,000 sq.ft.

Typically it would take **at least 2 months to do a 5-minute animation, and the client had only 15 days.** I asked them a few questions, and when I got my answers (**this is the importance of asking the right questions,** as I shared earlier), I committed to them a date and then delivered an almost impossible task on time.

It was a BIG project for me and led to an even bigger project, the NHPC, building a 3000 Mega Watt Concrete Gravity Dam and they wanted to develop mountains and the Dam in 3D, based on actual drawings. Never afraid to take up a challenge **and always eager to add value and provide solutions to my clients, I managed that as well.**

Then it was NTPC, BMW, Airport Authority of India and Amazon India and Next Design, and I was on a roll.

All this came about because I love helping people come out of challenging situations. I realized my dream of doing big projects has come true and destiny wants me to continue.

The universe then brought me the challenge of creating new bathroom designs every day. To help Bathroom Fitting brands break the jinx of being stuck at a few thousand followers and unable to leverage social media for marketing and profitability.

The challenge was to create content and designs that are unique, different and **"likeable", designs which add value and trigger emotions in the viewer.**

That was my introduction to Instagram, and it proved to be **a complete Game-Changer for me and the Bathroom brand client.**

Trying to find a solution to this challenge, I researched deeply, and I realized all Bathroom Fittings brands have a similar pattern. I decided to analyze it and find solutions by asking the right questions and shifting the lens.

I am sure you are now eager to turn the page and learn how to fast-track your social media onto the path of success at formula-one speed. Let's get this party started, then....

-5-

Are Videos Magical?

"Motion is not always the way forward; sometimes it pays to be still."

-Nitin Gupta, Out-of-the-box Design Thinking Expert

In my research journey, I studied multiple social media accounts in the Bathroom Fittings industry. After studying them, I found that the content that is posted falls into 2 main categories and then broadly into 15 subcategories.

The two main categories are:

1. **Video Reels**
2. **Still Image Posts**

In this chapter, I am sharing with you in detail about these two main categories, whether they work or not, and why.

Video Reels

These reels depending on the content and its intent can be of various types, such as

a. **Brand Videos-** These are great tools worth pushing and promoting; unfortunately, they cost a bomb, and hence it's not possible to make 100s of them. Due to this limitation, brand videos do not work out in our favor from the context of creating content regularly to bring us, followers in abundance continuingly.

b. **Infographics-** This is perhaps the most popular form of presenting content. Taking a product image and panning it with some text and music is a video that is considered an infographic. Though it fits well in the media plan, there are many parameters to check on this.

Is it a jaw-dropping video evoking positive emotions?

When even full-fledged 100 crore movies flop despite having the best directors, script, planning and professional actors. Do you think these infographics are going to bring us, followers? We believe we are showcasing the features of our products, and that's what the audience loves.

WRONG!

That's what YOU love! The product is your baby; no one is interested in your product until you show them how it impacts and adds value to their lives! **If showing product infographics could gain followers, your brand followers would be a million by now.**

Here's a tip:

If at all you want to convey product features, convey them as a still post.

At least while scrolling, people will see them. The video posts' thumbnails are not inviting and curiosity-provoking enough to open. And once opened, the videos are not exciting enough to be liked. The slides move too fast and hence are not even readable. **So, the whole intent of showing the features to the audience is wasted, along with the budget, of course.**

c. **Exhibition Videos-** These are videos to create awareness amongst your audience that you participated in a particular expo or trade fair, or any other industry event. These are good to have but they can't be expected to bring loads of followers.

d. **Architect and Interior Design Office Videos-** If your audience is architects, it's a good ego-massager. But honestly, no direct consumer is coming to social media to look at architect offices. So, this definitely does not fit the list of prospective tools that could get us followers.

e. **Sponsorship Videos-** A lot of time, Bathroom Fitting brands sponsor important and popular T.V.

shows to create brand awareness. Later they share the same videos on their social media in abundance. This has no significant positive impact and only steals the brand's identity and uniqueness.

f. **Influencer Videos-[Working to some extent]-** Agencies use Influencers because they have good followership. It is a trend to post videos of influencers, but the engagement that happens is very superficial.

   Most people are interested in the influencer and not your brand. Everyone knows these are paid partnerships, so the credibility quotient is low. The shelf life of such videos is significantly less. Also, the cost of influencers can't be ignored. A good influencer usually charges in lacs for a single post. That's no mean amount, and it's not a sustainable method.

   Also, I've seen people coming up with obscene comments, especially with female influencers. If, as a brand, you ask them to wear sexy dresses and make sexy poses, you are inviting the wrong audience. That audience will not stay with you or buy from you. **You don't want to build that kind of audience, do you?**

g. **Creative Contests- Dance/Music Videos** – Contests are exciting and fun, and these have the possibility to work. But it takes a lot of time, energy, and motivation for a common person to get up and participate.

Not many people are good at dance/music, and the percentage is even smaller of those who would like to make their profile public. It is a very tough task for any contest to go viral. I do not deny the possibility, but it's like a lottery. All a game of chance!

All of my clients have posed the same question to me,

"All agencies promise to create video content, but why aren't videos working the magic we expect, the magic agencies promise?

There are 3 primary reasons for that!

1. Today people are watching more video content than ever in the history of mankind. They have easy and cheap access to platforms like Netflix, Amazon Prime, and Disney Hot star. These platforms create excellent content, with top directors, actors, teams and tons of money on each video. Then also, a lot of videos fail. The videos made in an office by a video editor using one image and some sliding texts are a sheer waste of time, energy and money for the brand.

   The **quality of the video** has to be really top-notch for people to like it.

2. The kind of videos that are liked are where you find something that your mind does not have on its hard disk. For example, you would like a video if you see a kid running on a treadmill in the reverse direction.

Someone standing on one finger, or a tiger caring for a deer and not eating it. **Something unusual that we don't expect to happen.** These are the videos that are liked most.

3. A video is a series of still images and creates an expectation in the minds of the viewer, something interesting will come, something wow will come. When they view it for a few seconds and realize nothing wow is going to come, they scroll further, and all this happens in less than 5 seconds. So 5 seconds is all you have to hook them.

Here's a piece of Million Dollar Advice

DO NOT MAKE VIDEOS; unless you have million-dollar budgets and you can make them like the Warner brothers. But even supposing you have those resources, it's not possible to produce so many videos. **It takes months to build and work on a video that produces results.**

STILL IMAGE POSTS have a **higher probability** of getting liked.

The probability with stills is 50-50. Either your audience would like it, or they would not like it. There is no 3rd option.

However, in a video, if your content is lame and your designer is not an expert, the probability of your audience not liking it goes up as high as 95-100%.

-5-

So, Should We Stay Still?

"Social media posts are not just pictures. They must add value to people's lives and engage with their emotions."

-Nitin Gupta, Out-of-the-box Design Thinking Expert

Still Posts

Okay, now we know that still posts have a higher probability of engagement compared to videos; let's get a deeper understanding of still images.

From all the research and experimenting, I discovered that content with still posts was of the following themes, whether they are working or not.

a. **Festivals-[Not working]**- India is such a diverse country. It has some festival or the other every day. We get bombarded with messages wishing us on WhatsApp, and we ignore them. In fact, we delete them, which becomes a waste of time and energy for the brand.

Similarly, there are posts wishing you on all social platforms. As a brand, it's wonderful to show that you are aware of that festival and respect it, and lovingly want to wish the people celebrating it. But it certainly is not going to bring you the volume of followers you seek.

b. **Environment-Friendly Posts–[Not Working]**- This is almost similar to what I said above.

   If your company is developing products which are environment friendly. It's commendable, as it's the need of the hour. We must share that with people, and it may work for you to an extent. However, from a general perspective, ask yourself, is that going to get you the truckload of followers you are looking for?

   The short and only answer is No.

c. **Specific Days- [Not Working]**- Chocolate day, dog day, cat day, friendship day, enemy day, sun day, moon day and every other day on the planet and all others you can't even imagine. Yes, go ahead and post, but it's the same issue again.

   We are flooded with such messages on our emails, WhatsApp and Instagram. If this were to get you the desired results, **you would have been at a million followers today.**

d. **Direct Product Launch Shots-[Not Working]-** Of course, it's a great idea to launch your product to your own audience at no cost. That's precisely the eventual goal that we have a million followers one day, and we launch a product at no cost to a million people and generate business out of it.

   But regrettably, the point is this specific product launch post right now with minimal followers will make no impact. Also, it will not help you attract any additional followers. A 3D Faucet photo or a toilet photo with some text could be a formality to launch, but it's not helping you.

   On a side note, I have also observed some brands trying cheap tricks. How may you wonder?

   Here's how- The regular flow of likes on the entire Instagram page is 40 likes, 98 likes, 60 likes, and suddenly there are 3 product launch posts, with 5,500 likes, 5404 likes and 5,113 likes, and then again, the 4th day the likes drop to 76, 84 around this range.

   This makes it so evident that the likes are manipulated and that my friend is such a spoiler and leaves a negative impression about the brand.

e. **Promoting Architects with their photos-[Not Working]-** That's a good way to ego-massage your audience. Everyone likes to see their photos and be promoted. So, this doesn't always work. It works based on the intent when you genuinely want to highlight someone doing great work or want to give a shout-out to new upcoming talent, but it doesn't qualify as content that can get you followers in bulk.

f. **Contests-[Working and Not Working both]-** It is exciting and easy to come up with ideas about creating contests, but unfortunately, engaging them and getting huge numbers is not easy. It's just not working in 90% of cases.

   The reason could be your content is not able to trigger the emotional side of the audience. It could be due to the theme or the prizes not being attractive enough, or you may not have communicated them in a quickly readable manner **(as the decision to scroll the thumb is made in fractions of a second).** If your contest **is able** to trigger an emotion in the audience, it may work. But then it has to **be very** well thought out, and at the end of the day, it is all a matter of chance.

g. **Sports-[Not Working]-** Sports are happening all around, whether it is cricket, football or hockey. And, of course, they are a great way to connect with your audience. However, these posts don't really give us any results; they consume our important visual space without adding any value to the viewer. A sports enthusiast would already be following the sports channels anyway.

h. **Actual bathroom pictures designed by architects & designers** – Yes, this is one type of post that is getting a better response than all of the above-mentioned types of posts.

   People have aspirations. They want to live in a better home and have a better bathroom. These bathroom designs **trigger their emotions and stoke their desires for a better lifestyle,** and our job is done.

By now, as a Bathroom Fittings business owner or brand manager, you must be wondering, "Okay, Nitin, so by now, you have clearly told us what won't work or what might work to a certain extent. But in truth, what we want to know is what works. You promised to show us how to fast-track our social media at formula one speed to leverage it for profitability. So tell us what works, what is the best solution?"

Okay, just a little more patience, my friends. In the next chapter, I will reveal the magic mantra to you.

-7-

3D Bathroom Inspirations: The Magic Mantra

A Picture, they say, is worth 1000 words.
I say a 3D Bathroom Inspiration is an
emotional connect worth millions.

-Nitin Gupta, Out-of-the-box Design Thinking Expert

Let me ask you something, and if you answer honestly, you'll get the solution to your problem.

- If you were not the Brand Manager/Owner of your brand, would you like to follow your brand on Social Media?
- If your answer is YES, then you should have over 100k followers.
- If your answer is NO, then you would be struggling with around 20-30k followers or even less.

If you are struggling with 20-30 K followers, it means that 90% of your content is not working.

When 90 % of your content is not working, the right question to ask is, why is everything failing?

Why are all attempts to try new content and new agencies failing?

This will lead you to another, perhaps most vital, question.

What is it that people like to see?

This is the exact question which led me to research, and I figured out the million-dollar answer.

This is the magic mantra validated by the success of a leading bathroom fittings brand with over 340k followers.

3D Bathroom Inspirations-[Works.Definitely Works]

Having worked with a reputed Bathroom Fittings brand to help create miracles in their social media following and engagement and growth I can guarantee you that **3D Bathroom Inspirations** is what truly works.

Also right now only one brand is using this pioneering strategy. The timing is perfect to begin using this and harness the early bird advantage before this too becomes a commodity.

It is always the visionaries and pioneers who make the most impact and receive the most benefits.

Opportunity is knocking on your door, so get up and open that door wide. Incorporate 3D Bathroom Inspirations in your social media content and you'll be amazed at your growth and jump in followers.

Don't just take my word for it; I am sharing with you below, in detail, why this works and why you must include them as the major component in your content mix:

Bathroom ideas are the starting point of your customer's buying journey.

When a person starts to think about buying a new home or renovating a bathroom, the first thing that comes to mind is how it would look.

This brings along with it many questions.

- Will I be able to make the bathroom of my dreams within my budget?
- My bathroom size is small. Is it still possible to make it look beautiful and spacious?
- I can't afford to hire an architect. Where do I get design inspiration from?

That's where your 3D Bathroom Inspiration content comes in and adds value to their lives by providing solutions. Additionally, it helps them in other ways.

1. People come to social media to escape their stress. These Inspirations act as a visual treat and refreshing agents.
2. **People don't like to be sold to. It is the customer who buys.** This is the golden rule of business. Thus, you are offering them choices by showcasing your product in the 3D dream bathroom. This way, you are not pushing them; instead, you are inspiring them.

The Top Benefits of 3D Bathroom Inspirations are:

1. The audience has proven and approved this form of content with intent, and numbers validate that.

2. Top of Mind Recall is very high when using this form of content as it leaves a visual imprint on your audience's mind.

3. This medium of content will surely bring you into your buyer's top 3 consideration list if you remain consistent in its use. As they say, a picture is worth 1000 words, let me rephrase it to say that a 3D Inspiration is worth a million words, it builds an emotional connect with your audience.

4. It offers the early mover advantage (only one brand doing it right now). Be the pioneer and the visionary to get astounding results.

-8-

Wrapping It Up In A Nut Shell

Now that I have shared with you the formula for speeding up your social media performance and profitability let us quickly recap our learning. To make it more **digestible,** here is a summary.

1. Intent drives the Content.
2. If we are not getting the right results in our lives, we need to look at the questions we are asking and come up with more powerful questions to get powerful answers.
3. Conscious Content that can bring us followers in abundance is:
   - **i.** Actual bathroom pictures with your products, designed by creative designers and architects, attract your audience.
   - **ii.** 3D bathroom inspirations have done marvelously well in getting followers in the fastest possible time as they add value to their lives.

  - **iii.** Influencers can help but keep in mind the cost/benefit/shelf-life ratio.

4. Content that is not helping and is a mere formality in our media plan is:

Festival posts, Sports posts, Specific Days posts, Environment-friendly posts, and Videos (except Brand Films) don't work.

5. This is a Strict No:

Direct single Product Shots & Infographic videos

-9-

Let The Journey Continue

There are so many other reasons and benefits of Bathroom Inspirations that I could have written a thick fat book on them. But I have kept it short and sharp so that you can start implementing it immediately to get on the fast track to social media success.

Inspirations have not just brought followers but have transformed social media into a revenue-generating engine for the leading brand which has implemented it.

I have shared the magic formula in this book. However, our journey together doesn't have to end here. If you are keen on taking your brand to the next level with more such creative tools/ideas, reach out and email me at ng@thenextdesign.com and we can together embark on your supersonic social media transformation journey from there.

P.S.: Despite a packed schedule, I promise my team and I will revert to you within 48 hours.

For more transformative content and out-of-the-box ideas, stay connected with us at:

- www.thenextdesign.com
- www.linkedin.com/in/thenextdesign/

www.ingramcontent.com/pod-product-compliance
Ingram Content Group UK Ltd.
Pitfield, Milton Keynes, MK11 3LW, UK
UKHW022007190726
13853UKWH00004B/1798

9 789355 544797